LOVE OR LUST

A Young Woman's Quest For Love

Written By Terri Guthrie

Radiance Publishing, LLC

Forest Park, GA 30297

Love Or Lust Copyright 2018 Terri Guthrie

All Rights Reserved. No part of this book may be reproduced in any form or by any means without prior consent of the Publisher. Visit our website at www.radiancepublishingllc.com

IBSN-13: 978-1-732-1181-3-3

ISBN-10: 17321181-3-2

Love is the greatest gift a man can give – Joyce Meyer

7/16/15

It was supposed to be a one-night stand, but they could not get enough of each other. Kelli and Tyrese had sex every day, sometimes several times a day, and it was so good too! They had been going for two months solid, and Kelli had never experienced this, with what she thought would last one night. Kelli knew Tyrese loved her, he told her many times that he loved how she tastes, and she told him that she loved how he did it, and how he caressed her breasts, as if he loved and cared for her, his hands fitted perfect, like a hand in a glove, he stroked them gently. Kelli loved when she would ride him, he always took control after only a few minutes it seems, and she was fine with that, in the beginning. He would stop to eat her out, and he would end up on top, but she was a rider now, no more just laying down there and getting fucked! Kelli has learned to take control, she gets on him, and puts it directly where she wants it go, then takes him on a ride through her waves. She wants him to feel her! Her heart racing, and adrenaline pumping, she speaks to him through this energy!. It breaks her heart as he did not listen to it, as Tyrese tells her "Listen bae, I want to keep this strictly sexual, with no feelings involved". "What the fuck?" Kelli replied, "I do not know how to do that". She became silent and grasped on to the thought that every time he enters her vagina, it touches her heart, and weakens her a bit. She thought, "it must weaken him as well, but he has up a mental block, or something that prevents him from feeling anything besides the lust from entering". How does he do that? She is back from her thought, when he says to her, "get out of your feelings". "Easier said than done, that takes time!" Kelli says. He begs her not to leave, after she threatens to cut him off. "If you want me out of my feelings, then we have to stop fucking", she said. He says that he just has trust issues, and that it is not her that he does not trust, but it is love, and the fact that he is so use to being used. Well, so is she, but she is willing to give love a try. They sit and talk about all the pain, and memories from past relationships, and how they both have been used before. They are becoming closer, with each story shared, they can relate to one another, but fear has him in a corner, with a knife to his throat, threating to kill him if he makes a move. He is hurting himself, and the woman he cares for, losing that fear will help him to open up! Tyrese tells Kelli, that he is trying, and she wants to believe him, but she stills feels that she should stop fucking and spending so much time with him to see what happens. This is different for her, this seems like a relationship, but he assures her that they are just friends, she is confused, but he is interesting, and she wants more.

718/15

"I am so horny", Kelli says to herself. As she sits and think about masturbation, something she has never been comfortable with, not only because her nails are long, but because she wants to be touched by a man, and feel him inside of her, but she was not calling Tyrese back, nope not today. He needs time alone to make up his mind, and so she did not call.

7/25/15

"Sex, I love head and sex", Kelli writes, "but I only want it with one person. Yeah, Tyrese fell in love, but it was with my sex. I want someone to fall in love with my mind, let us have mind sex, I want to fall in love mentally, and get my mind gone, and blown. Let's get to know each other. Our bodies may very well have the urge, but if our mental does not connect, then we are just cut buddies, you know, in this for the sex, and that is the one thing that I do not want! I want someone to love me, and I love them, their personality, and overall well being; them, just for who they are. I believe that people just want to be accepted, and that is where the fear of being themselves comes from. They are afraid that people will not like them, but no matter what we do, or who we are, someone will always have an opinion, whether it be good or bad, and that is why we should not look to please people, but I wanted to please Tyrese, and we should do whatever make us happy, rather people like it or not. May God bless them all, especially the haters, because they need God the most. All people are not necessarily haters just because they do not like something, for example, my sister had her hair done in a mullet, short at the top and long in the back, a style I know from the early 90's. I told her it was cute on her, because her face is cute and she can rock any style. I did not like that style for me, but she rocked it with a smile, and I was proud of her for not allowing me not liking her hairstyle to get her down, not that I was trying to. She could accept the fact that we all have different taste in style. I believe we all must learn to embrace our differences, and complement one another, and receive positive criticism without getting upset and out of character, just like my sister did".

7/26/15

Kelli writes, "I think that I am just in love with the feeling of being in love. I want a true love relationship. I love Love".

"My first love, what most would call puppy love, (an informal feeling of love), was wonderful. He and I would talk about our future together, and life at that moment. I really loved him and felt that he really loved and cared for me, he told me and showed me. I haven't found another like him yet. He was so sweet, and nice, and kind to me. He kept it real, he told me the truth whether it would hurt me or not, but he did it tactfully and with care. Our relationship was not like any other that I have had to this day. I only dream about how it would be if he and I were currently together. I miss his lips, his touch, and his brain, conversation wise, and down below. What ever happened to good conversation? Not just about sex, but dropping knowledge and wisdom on each other, massages, walks, sitting and talking about everything, being romantic, all in love and not worrying about anything. Oh, how I miss him? I want love. He must be respectful, caring, trustworthy, nice looking, financially stable, and clean, especially his teeth".

7/27/15

So, she dated this guy, you know, the one where it was supposed to be a one -night stand, yea, him, Tyrese, who was angered one day by the fact that she liked him and wanted to be more than just friends, it has been a few days away from three months since they met. She was in love with a man who refused to fall in love with her, he runs and hides when it gets too deep, then talks his way back in, when she says that she is done, every time he tells her to get out of her feelings, she tells him to stop fucking her as often and as good as he did. "Look at how long we have been fucking, do you not feeling anything?", Kelli asked. She thought to herself, "What a shallow heart he must have, or is it a broken heart as he claims? Does he feel rushed?" If so, he should, because she is rushing, she wants him to hurry up and fall in love with her, so she can stop the search. Her motives are all wrong and maybe he can see that, so he is not willing to give in. She must first find out why she really wants him. Is it love, or lust, or just sadness? She found someone who showed a little interest, so she wants to keep him, and he obviously wants to be kept, or he would not come over, as often as he does, but she is forceful, and dominating, and he does not like that. Some men like to be in control, but she was the controlling one, so used to running things, being a boss, and a leader, and she is now realizing her ways. She must learn to keep calm, and allow her man to lead at times, he is not a sheep, although he may wonder off at times, which is very well needed, but when he returns, it will be like a new love, only thing is, Tyrese was not her man, but she wanted him to be, and she fucked him like he was. He said that it was only his sex that she was attracted to, but that was not true, because he came extremely fast most of the time when they have sex, and blamed her that day, saying to her that her pussy too good, and true enough it is very good, so she takes the blame. Somehow, Kelli found herself taking the blame for a lot in this "relationship", to avoid arguments, but he would get upset about everything. He got upset about which pump she should park at, at a gas station the other day, so of course she just parked where he wanted her too, if the spend limit was 35 and she was going 36, he would be so fueled with anger at her for going too fast, like damn nigga, are you riding dirty? When they were engaging in sex one night she moaned too loud and he got mad at that, "you cannot take dick", he told her, she would usually talk shit, but this time said nothing, instead, she wanted to show him that she could take dick, they fucked again, all night, he went hard, and she let him know, he was the man, she did not talk back, instead she showed him, by taking it. Everything she did irritated him, and he told her that. He told her that she asks too many questions, being nosey, and wanting him all to herself, that she was being selfish. He said that he was just playing when he said that she irritated him, but she thought, "maybe I should leave this guy alone". Her breaking point was when she texted him after not talking for a few days. She texted, "hey baby", he texted back saying, "Bitch do not call me your baby", and threatened to shoot her, it was over after that, she did not respond, but he kept calling and texting her, right after, saying that he was just playing. She believes he realized that he had just lost a good woman. She never responded, blocked his number and went on with her life. She thought a lot about what he told her about himself, and she came to realize that he had a lot going on in life and that is it was not her that he was mad at, or upset with, but that it was his self. She believes he wants more out of life but is just too afraid to step out and get it, or he does not know how to go about getting whatever it is that he wanted, or it might be that he does not know what it is that he wants. He just knows that he is not happy with what he has right now, so he would make up lies about having a job, and his own place, and even joked around about being married, and wanting to sleep with her sister. Who does that? Kelli was imagining him to be what she wanted him to be. "It is not right to play games with one's heart, just because you are hurting", Kelli said. "I think we need a break from each other", is what Tyrese said. She thought that he was fearful that love will take over him, and make him weak, he refused to let her touch his heart, so to keep it cold, he keeps love at a distance and if he feels it coming on he stops it immediately! To stop love you simply do not accept it, by being mean to whomever is trying to give it to you, and if that person see it, then they will leave you alone, or fall back a little, because love hurts. As she sits and thinks, she wants to cry out so loud, and scream and shout to the mountain top, as she is already doing so inside. She did not want to be in love with him, and still, only her heart hears her, but her heart does not care, it wants what it wants, when it wants it, her heart is was troubled, her mind must step in to help her to get over it, because her heart does not listen. He is brutally honest as he sits her down and explain to her, that he is a bad guy, and that he is not good for her, but he does not see what she sees, she is looking too deep and missed some of what he was saying. She did not care, she wanted a bad guy so that she could try and tame him.

Hell, at this point Kelli just wanted to be in love, as long as it was real, and he loved her back, "if I can feel it, it was real to me, me being able to actually feel loved, I see it", she thought to herself. She listened to him, and wanted him more, after hearing some of the things he told her he has done, she was turned on by his courage. "It is cool", she says, then kisses him, and he gave her more of him, she loved to feel him inside of her, he said bend over, and so she did.

7/27/15

I love love, but love does not love me, it runs and hides; while I seek earnestly to find, the games it play with my heart, are one of a kind; and I am the joker at mind; simply because it fools me every time. It makes me see things that are not there; feel things and expect that they feel it too. Love has blinded me, Eve was right! I am so blacked out, with no light in sight. I have fell so deep into it. The only way out is to stand on all this BS that love has me in a trans about! Oh, I just wanted love to love me back, do not push me away and never come back. I want to be close to you, not closed to you. Open me up like a door without hinges. I am not going to continue to be deceived, I want you love, but you have not believed. Love, love me back.

7/30/15

"Sometimes, I want to go back to that mentality I had when I was a stripper", Kelli thought out loud, "I did not put up with broke flexing ass niggas. You could not even see me up close if you did not have any money! I did not need or want for anything! Nigga say he wants to buy me a drink, "nigga I will buy you, and the whole fucking bar!" I was the finest thang walking around, I would smile, then shake my ass, and do a trick on the pole, and money would be everywhere, sometime even before I took my attire off. I had all the attention, "hey baby", they would say, "damn who dat?", like they are cheering for the Saints. I did not care, as long as you came to spend that check, let me see that cash, and I would dance for you all night long, even talked dirty to you. Hell, I was not looking for love, I was looking for help, and that money really helped me out a lot, I miss it at times, but I cannot go back, to that "fuck you pay me, niggas ain't shit" mentality, my heart was not there. I still get paid though!"

8/4/15

Kelli is so in love with the Weekend's song "Earned it", it makes her so wet, his voice alone, oh, and Jeremiah's voice.

Jeremiah's song "birthday sex", was her theme song back when she was dancing. "Earned it", made her want to suck dick with ice that day, and so she did. Avant loved it! She went to see him, since Tyrese was acting stank these past few days. Avant was funny, he played "earned it", on repeat all night, they drank, Kelli only smoked weed around him, because he supplied it, and she was not really a smoker, she was lit that night, and he was loving it every second of it, he said so himself. If Tyrese would be her man, she would do that for him every day, and whatever else he wanted!

Kelli just wants love, to be in love and be loved back. She wants him to fall so deep in love with her that he cries, and he will have a reverential fear of her, meaning that he loves her so much that he will do what he needs to do to not displease her, and her the same for him. She does not want him to be afraid of her, but to trust her with his heart, she wants him to give it to her just as fast as he gives cash to the cashier on Saturday morning for them fresh J's. He says he gone buy her some J's, she said fuck him and those J's, Kelli could buy them if she wanted to, but she does not wear J's, she likes Nike's, Air Max, and anything cute.

8/5/15

"I will no longer be controlled by food, I ate this huge cookie, because it was good, and I wanted to, but I really did not want to, I did it due to lack of self-control, and even though I feel like I have to vomit, I want to finish it off. God please help me to not be a prisoner of junk food, or food period. Help me to eat only when I am hungry, and to eat right". Thank you, love Kelli.

"As we lay here Tyrese is holding me in his big strong arms, my frame fits perfectly, as I push up against his body. We are a perfect match, made in heaven, literally. He must be heaven sent, or it would not be what I want! Why else would he keep coming back? He teaches me, and I teach him. We grow together and are building this fantastic relationship. I love when we lay there, and he talks to me about what is on his mind. He says, "Tell me you love me! I already know you do, why will you not say it?" Kelli said, "I do not love you, I like you a lot, why do you want me to say that". "Because it is true", he said. Kelli said nothing, and he back in it, from the side. This morning Kelli told him, "I love you". Tyrese said, "I already know you do, I love you too". According to Kelli, she been knowing that too.

8/7/15

Leave your fears and worries behind you. What do you think about that makes you happy? Why do you not do it, is it realistic? I am not going to point out every single mistake a person makes, we are all human, and pointing out everything someone does wrong can really hinder that person, and lower their self-esteem in doing things, and makes you look like a hypocrite, or a hater. It makes the assumption that you do not make mistakes, it is nerve wrecking, unprofessional, and inconsiderate. You must learn to encourage yourself and others, especially while you are going through it, whatever "it" may be. "As I sit here, I wonder if sometimes the "it" that we are going through is something we want to go through. Do we create these "its" for ourselves, so that we can relate to being or feeling down, and so that we are able to pick ourselves back up? Love- oh sweet four-letter word, why do you not love me? My heart aches for you, I want you so badly, I will do whatever you want me too, just show me you want me like how I want you. Pick me up and carry me, hold me tightly in your arms, feast on me, like a newborn latched to his mother's nipple, sucking her sweet natural milk. I know you will find me naturally, because I am naturally for you, I can feel it. Why must you deceive me and play with my heart, like a harp playing a slow long painful song, piercing my ears, and my heart. Taking out my heart and tossing it up and down, from the air. No way Jose', that is not fair!

8/8/15

Questions

How often do you challenge yourself, and in what ways? What do you think about when you are alone? How do you handle criticism? Do you accept constructive criticism? Are you easily angered by it? Are you truthful with yourself? Do you know who you are? Why are you on earth? Do you believe everyone has a purpose in life, rather it be good or bad? Are you a forgiving person? What frustrates you? What makes you happy, really happy? What are you looking for in life? Do you look to things to make you happy, or does happiness come from within? What do you do for you? "When will I start working for myself?" Kelli thought, "I will push myself as hard as I do while working for someone else!"

8/9/15

"I refuse to let trials and tribulations steal my joy or dictate my future. I will be glad and rejoice in every trail, thanking God all the way through it, because I know that when I get to the other side of this trial, there will be a great blessing for me, rather it be strength, courage to get through, the practice of perseverance, a newfound joy, or deeper trust in God. I know that God will make good out of this regardless of how it may look now. God knows way beyond my understanding. I will not let it steal my smile, my peace, change my mind, my mood, or my attitude. I may think a bad thought, but I have the right to choose what I want to think; therefore, I can choose to think a good thought, and empty out that bad thought like a full bag of trash, just take it out; it might leave a little drip behind, but nothing that cannot be cleaned and mopped up".

8/11/15

"Why do I always do this to myself, it is as if I cannot recognize the difference between reality and my emotions. It appears I really feel it, but it is never really real. I fall for the same men every time. Why can't I have someone that would want me as deep as I want them. I think it is because maybe it is not really them that I want, but love. So desperate, for love and acceptance, I would easily be led astray, allowing my heart to deceive me, I know better! Even though I know I am beautiful, if I heard it from a man I was feeling, it was like magic, he could have me in love so deep. I think that is all I really want, an intimate, deep relationship. I heard to get something you never had, you have to do something you have never done, but I am trying new things all the time, and I am still single. I just want his attention again but fuck him".

8/11/15 pm

Tyrese

Kelli was not feeling him after a while, but still tried to make him fall in love with her. Why? She does not know, and it did not work out that way for her either, he ended up hating her so much. He even threatened to have his sisters jump once, and said that he will shoot her, for the second time. Damn! That is the total opposite of what Kelli was going for. He was a bit difficult to deal with, but as time went by, they carried on. Things slowed down, and they ended up fucking only four times a week. He came so fast each time, it was not satisfying, but he swore that his dick had her sprung, and made her go crazy. Laughing hella hard. So, her wanting his heart, went along with it, she did not tell him that his dick was not so good, in fact, Kelli wanted a man so bad, she did just the opposite. She told him, "yes baby, you should not have given it to me like that, had me moaning and screaming like that". She was just loud , he got mad, and said, "you cannot take dick", "no, baby it just feels good", Kelli said. Which was true that time, while it lasted, she continues, "I want you to know you doing a good job". She did go ahead and tell him that he comes too fast, but she had told him that many times before. He still mad, then blames her again, saying this time her pussy is too wet and good. Kelli had never heard anything like that before, this must be the right path, and so she agreed. Later on that day, when they had sex, she did not get loud, nor did she tell him how good he made her feel, she rode him and he nutted instantly. She had just got up there, went up and down, a few times and he was done, moaning the whole little while, and he nutted all inside of her, but that was her man. Kelli told Tyrese that she wanted to go again, and they always do, it is longer the second round, he nuts again, while he is on top this time. He sees that she is not happy and then tell her again her pussy is whack. Kelli laughed at him, she knew he was mad, because just yesterday and earlier, it was too wet and good, and all because he cannot keep his dick up long enough for her to get a good nut. Out of the times they had sex, she came only a few good times, all the other times he would come right before she is about to, she figures he thought he made it up by letting her ride his face. He taught her a new way to ride his face, but still, it is not the same. He says, "that is why I nutted in you, and you are going to take care of my baby by yourself". "Boy bye, you will leave me to take care of your child by myself"? Kelli questioned. He laughed it off, "no I will take care of my baby, and keep fucking you". "Whatever", is what she said. She stayed around, hoping he would love her, but she was so naive, so blind to the fact that she was living in a fantasy world, and that he did not give two fucks about her. He would say that he worked, and went to school, had his own place, same as her. They would talk about her day at work, and school, he would talk about school, but would get upset asked about his work. "I think he just hates his job, or maybe he was just angry about something in his life that had nothing to do with me, or work. Or maybe he was mad at me", Kelli thought to herself. She googled his named and his arrest record popped up, she was not surprised because he had already told her about it. But she saw something that caught her eye, it said that he was once arrested for allegedly physically abusing someone, who had a restraining order on him, and that he was arrested again for violating that order. Kelli being Kelli, asked him about it, because he told her everything else, and she had questions. He was nice enough to answer them for her. He explained what happened, and she understood, because that has happened to her before, but he lied so much, she never knew what to believe anymore.

8/13/15
"Pussy ass niggas hate my blood, I grind and work hard to get mine, and they hate it! I can see it in their eyes, that is why they gets no attention from me, I stay to myself, and mind my own business".
8/20/15
"Day eight of my diet, and I am doing good, besides the chocolate covered peanuts, which are not bad, is what I tell myself. My diet consists of no candy, low carbs, no bread, no pasta, and no soda, it has been tough, but I am learning to resist temptation, plus I look good in my clothes".

8/21/15 rolling into 8/22/15
"Why must I always play the foot, I know better! I just wanted to go out and have a good time, drink a little, fuck Tyrese good, and get

some money. No, I do not fuck for money, but if you are fucking me, you are going to cash out, because I will do the same for you, he usually comes through for me, but not this day. My sister shared her drink with me, after I stopped by there, but before even stopping over my sister's house Tyrese and I had plans on hanging out that night, when I got out of school. We had been texting each other all day. He told me he was around the corner, and to get ready, so I get ready. I called him 40 minutes later, after I was ready, he says that he is downtown, and that he will be leaving in five minutes, then hung up on me, that is the last I heard from him that night, or maybe even period, who knows, my phone will be off tomorrow anyway, because he was going to pay my phone bill. I do not know how I forgot to include my phone in budgeting, maybe because I did not budget this month. I am so hurt; my heart is heavy and full of pain. I want someone to want me, to care about me, and to be in love with me, someone I can feel the same way about. I am so done with these messy ass, no good men. I am always fooled, they seem so cool in the beginning, then they stop. I want attention, if you want me, tell me, if you care, say it, but he does not, and it shows. I do not feel loved or cared for, my heart is not broken, because I know I deserve better, and I will have better, it is just the "right now" that irks me, I think I have to have it all, right now!"

Kelli deleted all the men that she was messing around with, well, really just two, out of her phone, that way, She is not going backward. She vowed to not text or call, because she will not have their numbers.

"These bitches fake, these niggas fake, motherfuckers ain't shit, but fucking liars. Fuck them all. I am tired of letting people hurt me. I do not want to be evil, but it looks like I am going to have to be. Or, wait, no, I'm not, I will just leave them alone, it is not like they fuck with me no way". Kelli was really digging this dude, but he is a liar, and plays too many games, it's sad. "I cannot sleep now, I have to let go and restock. Those lovers have expired, time for new ones".

8/22/15

"Wow, so Tyrese called me all night, but I am not surprised at all, I am a good woman. Here we go again. He can have a good heart when he wants too. He has been calling since the 18th, but this night I decided to answer, just to hear his voice, and it was the same, that same tone of game, and I sensed anger. Why is he so mad, angry, and full of rage? Is it jealousy? He cannot even fuck, I would not fuck him again. He comes too quick, I never get my nut like how I want, but he always gets his. I was only feeling him because to me he looked like my favorite rapper, but he does not even have enough stamina to be "Bad Ass", he is such a broke little liar, fuck him".

8/23/15

Random Thought

Have you ever daydreamed with your eyes open, so deep in your dreaming you thought your eyes were closed? In your mind, you are looking at it, and see it so clear, only to snap back and realize that you were staring right at the nothing.

Have you ever had a feeling about something so strong that your body starts to react to it as though it were actually happening? I made myself cum today, without even touching myself, wow!"

8/31/15

So, Saturday night 8/29/15, Kelli decided it was time to go see Tyrese, after this entire time of him begging, they were back and forth, she will block and delete him, but always let him back in. He tells her that they are slowly, very slowly working on getting to know each other better, she said okay, and listened to him talk. They ended the night with a kiss and a nice long hug. She did not want to let him go, he smelled so good.

8/31/15

Late night sex talk

She sees his name light up across the screen:

"Hello, Kelli says in her soft, sexiest, most seductive way, that come fuck me right now voice!

"Hey baby, I miss you, been thinking about you all day, and watching that video you sent me over and over, made me miss you more baby, I jacked off to it twice", Tyrese says. "I knew you would love it" she replied. He continued, "I love how you spread those pretty pussy lips apart, I saw me kissing it nice and slow, then faster, pulling you closer into my face. Damn baby, the way you got my dick hard as a brick right now, I can hear you saying my name, say my name". Kelli moaned "Oh Tyrese! I miss you too baby, I thought about you so much my panties were soaked, I had to share with you, how you made me feel. I felt you, even though you were not around. I wish I could come to you right now and ride all night long, your face and dick, until I shake and come, I got some things I want to show you. Then you turn me over, and beat it like I owe you money, then kiss it and make sweet love to it, fucking me so right, with deep long strokes, tease me with just the tip a little, I like that, then twist, turn and bend me in every way I will go. Oh, I am getting wet right now just thinking about it baby". He says "Damn baby all that, just unlock the door, I am on my way to you. I cannot wait no more. I want to feelme inside of you right now, that is my warm, tight and tasty pussy. I can see me now sucking all your sweet juices like I was dehydrated, and this was the only fountain left. I want to go so hard for you, because I know you will go hard for me baby". She says, "let's fall in love". He says "hum, well, we can see where it leads too". Kelli laughs quietly in her head, men hate that love word, unless it has something to do with sports, food, sex, or money, they love that all day then, but no female. Maybe it is fear. But anyway, she just says okay, and hang up. She carried on about her night, and about how tomorrow will be an opportunity to have an even better day, even though today was great, still things to accomplish. She really felt that this conversation had taken place, but it was all a dream, the whole thing.

9/2/15

1 Corinthian 3:16

Do you not know that you are the temple of God?

Ecclesiastes 3:3

For a dream comes through the multitude of business; and a fool's voice is known by multitude of words.

9/2/15

"I think I am a nympho, I love having sex, I am always horny, always! I want to fuck even right now, that is why I need a man, so, I can get it on a regular with one person and fall in love", Kelli writes. So, she had sex today with Grimms, aka no good, why can she notstop thinking about sex, it is sickening, but anyways, this time was cool, different from the other times, maybe because this time they did not make it to her bed, they fucked right there on the couch and standing up on the living room floor, it was nice, longer than usual. He fucks too much, Kelli could tell, (look who's talking). She met Grimms in traffic, he is just someone she uses mainly for when she needs some extra money in her pocket, they fuck sometimes, but he has agirl. They had been fucking months before she met Tyrese. In the beginning, Kelli had to go off on Grimms about the money, he would try to $40 dollar her, but he has learned better, and he always comes through, with whatever she asks for. Grimms even bought her baby a bike for her birthday, and he never even met her. Kelli told him, that this was the first and the last time she will ever fuck him again, without him going downtown and licking her sweet pussy. He just smiled, he lucky it was just supposed to be a "quickie". This nigga was moaning louder than her, but she enjoyed it too, her mind was on Tyrese. She met Tyrese while she was on the phone with Grimms one day, going into her apartment, Tyrese asked for her number, she gave it to him, and told him to call her. Kelli went inside her apartment. Tyrese called right away, she got off the phone with Grimms, and stepped back outside, to see what was up with Tyrese. They talked for ten minutes or so, but she was ready to go inside, so he called on the phone, and they talked until dawn. "I wish Tyrese could go as long and as hard as Grimms did, I would love it, but truth be told, I love all my men, Avant too." She met Avant through social media, but he lived around the corner, close by Tyrese mother's house. Avant was a cool dude, he was funny, and they got fucked up together, he re-introduced her to weed, they jammed every now and then. This fool tries to play on her intelligence, laughing Hella hard, he thinks she does not know, he is nothing but a hoe, this nigga stays on lame as social sites, he got some good ass head, but Kelli does not want him though. So, with all three of her men combined, she has a good man. She feels she just need two more, a baller, and one that will just fall head over heels in love with her, and her the same with him. That is her ultimate goal, love. She wants to give love and receive it. Kelli feels a lot of relief when she writes, it is a stress reliever. "It is not what you do, it is how you do it. "I have my own technique of writing", Kelli says. Her thoughts come so fast sometimes, she may be on one subject, then her mind jumps to another, so she leaves to turn the page and write it down, before she forgets, then once it is written, she may go back to what she was writing about, or move on. She writes, "call it impulsive writing or whatever, that is my style, it is what makes me different from other writers. And there is nothing wrong with being different"! But fuck all these men!

Females are so funny, everyone wants to compete. Honey I am not in competition with anybody. I just want to be successful in life, I do not care what you do not like about what I do, or how I look, or any of that. I am going to continue to live my life the way I want, progressing daily, making improvements on areas that I know need improving. Working and accomplishing goals, learning daily what to do, and what not to do. My mom taught me a long time ago, that I did not have to be seen and heard, and still this day, I hung on to it, because the loudest girls have the lowest self-esteem. I can walk into the room without saying anything, and all eyes are on me, because pretty does not have to announce its presence. At times, I hope that no one sees that my confidence is not so high, not until, I am happy with how I look. I feel sometimes how can I expect someone else to be happy with me, I must first love me and my body before he can. I need to work out more and eat less crap, I weight 140, but I feel 340, I need my energy back"!

"I know what I want, and what to do to get it, so why am I so disobedient? Do I really want this? I am fine, but I can be finer, I just do not want all of that attention, I get enough of it walking around in scrub pants and a t shirt, Lord knows I really am going to be feeling all over myself, when I get this body how I want it, and my man will be able to enjoy it as well. My clothes will look even better, I need help shopping for clothes, I always pick the same things, but I did start wearing skirts, and dresses".

9/2/15

Kelli wants to write and express everything, some personal, and some to share. She says to herself, "Do not be afraid; fear not, express yourself, be honest, take control of the words on the paper, you create your journey, branch out. Fear not, write about whatever you want to write about, so what if someone finds out, to hell with them, write a book if you want. Do not expect to have a private life if you do decide to share anything, you will be judged, criticized, and talked about in many ways".

9/2/15

"Why is he so afraid of me?", Kelli questioned, "I knew he was, but him admitting it to me made me think about a lot of things I have felt that he thought. These things I think are coming true, I said that he was afraid of me, he did not specify why, but I know it is because he really wants to love me, but he is afraid of getting hurt, and he is intimidated by my drive to succeed. I want to sit down and talk business relationships, goals, and everything with him, maybe he is not the one. I am not sure, but I feel a strong urge for him. Little do he know, I can be under his control like he wants, if he knew how to handle me, but

he is just like a lot of men, cannot handle such a strong woman, who really does not need them, but just wants them.

But why do I want him? He is evil, no I take that back, he is not evil. Maybe I am moving too fast, but to me, if someone likes me, they would want to spend time, and make more time for me, but that is not the case here. So, why do I chase him, maybe I want to chase him away, but I do not. I want him to want me. I like a challenge, but this is real, even when he chases me back, but this time, I do not think he wants me and I need to move on, rather than dwelling on it. I do not need to think too hard about it, because it will give a chance for him to reel me back in. It is what it is. Get over it and move on. God has something better in store for you, do not miss out on your blessing, chasing a mess that you do not need, girl you are just horny, is what I tell myself. Do you really feel anything when you all are fucking? Be honest, No. You are just so desperate for love, that you are willing to settle for what you know you do not want and you know that you can do better, and that you deserve better, so, just delete his number, that is the only way for you not to contact him, because he hardly ever calls you anymore, and he only text when he wants some head, or some pussy. He previously said it was not good, but be all up in it, moaning like all he in love, and get mad when you do it. Why do you have sex? That is a question that I was once asked in class? I said for pleasure, and for love. So, ask yourself the same question. "Why do you have sex"? and be honest, rather it be for money, entrapment, escape, pleasure, food, clothes, bags, whatever your reason. Is it worth the risks involved; feelings, risks for STD's, especially without condoms, and yes, things can be caught even when wearing a condom; genital warts, herpes, crabs, and with kissing, you can get herpes.

9/9/15

"Today was a great, yet stressful, and hectic day. I went to work today, after dropping my kids, and my sister off to my other sister's spot. I stayed at work until ten a.m., then went to planned parenthood, awaiting my results from my STD testing, which were negative for chlamydia and gonorrhea, HIV, and syphilis, I let my men know these results, I texted Tyrese first, because we fuck unprotected still. I was curious to know why it was burning when I go to urinate. The nurse practitioner gave me antibiotics for bacterial vaginosis and ran a herpes test. After leaving the doctor, I went to the dentist, because my mouth hurts, and I cannot eat, which is kind of good, because I am sort of on a diet, but anyway, at the dentist she was a young black doctor. I was happy to see her, she gave me hope and motivation, just doing what she does, and I was taller than her, which was cute. But she gave me some antibiotics, mouthwash, and some pain cream, and steroid cream. I am feeling much better already. Oh, I did not mention that the nurse practitioner went ahead and gave me a prescription for herpes, just in case, and I started taking them today already. The doctor I work for gave me sixteen Tylenol's with codeine, whereas normally, the nurse would give me thirty, he was just being petty. It is really time for me to move on from there, my time was up a longtime ago, why am I holding on, I do not know. It is a lot of things I need to go ahead and let go, get rid of, but I allow fear and/or laziness to hold me back. Time for change, I will consider this day a wakeup call, and on top of leaving work early, I found out that I just got 60 cents raise. Yaay!

I have two assignments from class.

Assignment number one. List five things you have failed to fully and completely admit or acknowledge to yourself.

- I really want my children to have a close relationship with their father
- If the youngest's father gets his act right, I will be with him.
- I want to become financially stable, and save, but I am too lazy to budget every month.
- I want to lose weight and get fit. I do not know why I am holding myself back.
- I really want to write a book, I need to stay consistent with my writings, it is hard to write fiction.

Assignment number two. What excuses do you tell yourself (Write a story) "The Story I Tell Myself" Be honest, you know your patterns, you know your typical excuses, rationalizations, and justifications for failure. Begin like this, I did not create a meaningful lasting change because… Be creative, honest, thorough, and blunt.

"What do you do or say to con yourself, and let yourself off the hook, when times get tough? Why do you suddenly quit, before you achieve what you want? Do you understand how to change the pattern? If you know which behavior gets which results, you eliminate the errors, and win.

-The story I tell myself when it comes to eating right and exercising.- I always have an excuse, excuses, excuses, excuses. When I choose to eat cookies, knowing I do not need to, and that I am not even hungry, the excuse I tell myself is that I am already fat anyway, no one cares, and maybe no one cares, because I do not care. If I took better care of myself and gave myself more respect, and really discipline myself, my life would be great. If I could give myself the advice that I would give others, life would be better. I often talk down to myself, if I want to do something that I know is not right, I will bring myself down to that level to excuse myself and say oh it is okay. I am a fat ass, I can never lose weight, just be downright negative towards myself, saying things that will make me feel horrible, and so now it is okay to eat what I want, that is the bs I tell myself, but I know I can be positive and do better, and lose weight, maybe it is just laziness, or being insecure. But I can be secure if I stop being lazy and making excuses for myself, and stop all of all this negative talk towards myself, because I am worth more than that. I will not be defeated by food, or anything. It does not rule me, nor will I let it control me any longer. I will resist temptation, although it may be hard, I have help. God has sent me a toothache, and mouth pain, to avoid these bad irritating foods that I do not need anyway. Thank you, Lord.

The story I tell myself when it comes to sex. I tell myself that he will fall in love with me after sex, so, I will sex him, hoping he will. Yes, he will come back, for sex, but, that is all. Because that is all I have offered. I have to be smarter than that, think higher than just sex, become friends, get to know each other, go out in public together, talk all day and night about every topic; subject, any and everything. Laugh together, share stories, happy, sad, funny, horrific, amazing stories, talk about what the good God has done for us. Find similar interest in things, and in each other. Make each other feel accepted and wanted, and needed, and cared for, and eventually loved. Show you care, be kind, and loving, use gentle words, be honest, not brutal, but tactful. Be yourself; there is no one else to be. Find out what you want in a person, and what they want. Spend time sharing memories, talk about plans, goals, wanted achievements, past achievements, what motivates us. Why are you determined to find love? I have been through a lot in life, and I want love because I think I need it. I need that feeling that someone, a man, cares for me and loves and wants me. I need his acceptance, and approval of me being me, without it there is no real relationship, I would want him to want the same from me. Our foundation must be strong before kids even join in. Then I say, Kelli, you are an amazing person, and it is okay to admit that. There is nothing wrong with being amazing, it is not bragging, or boasting; do not look at it that way. Do not listen to those negative thoughts, and people, telling you that you are not amazing, because of what you do not know, or do not do. You are an amazing, great, and unique person, because God says so, and you know you are, so stop putting yourself down and trying to beat yourself up. Let your amazingness show, smile, continue to be happy. Do not down play your emotions, because you are around a bunch of sad, miserable people. Be that shining light in a room, or where ever you go. Just because you work and go to school with negative people does not mean you have to be negative, or feel bad for being happy, and overjoyed around them, maybe they will cheer up a bit, when they see how happy you are, so, do not allow others to change you, your attitude, your emotions, your focus, be determined to succeed, because you will overcome all that they throw your way. Greater is He that is in me, than he, that is in the world. Use your powers and go get what you dream. It is yours, you just have to press on, and not give up, not allow others nor yourself, to deter you away from your goals, regardless of the reasonings.

How do you feel about yourself?

9/24/15

Kelli does not know her worth, so she moves fast and try to make him fall in love with her sex, she does not know her potential. She refused to believe that she deserves better, she downgrades to make herself feel better. The truth is blinded in her mind, her imagination has taken over, she only views the world in her own thoughts with disregard to what the facts are. She believes whatever she wants, as anyone should, but why not believe the best, even if the worst happens, just know that it is preparing her for something better, then her puny imaginations are willing to seek. She is afraid of heights, so she thinks low thoughts. Daydreaming about all the horrible things that will happen if she was to find a man, daydreaming about how he will hurt her instead of love her, but can you blame her, she has never experienced real love. She reflects on what she knows, and what she has been through, rather than moving on. She is still hurt from the pain of the past relationship with her youngest child's father, and until she admits the truth, it will continue to eat her up, literally, she eats up everything, and when she is full she is still looking for more. Stress eating, mistaking emotional hunger for actual physical hunger, is causing her to gain unwanted weight. When will she learn? Do not be hindered by your mind Kelli.

Good news, her herpes results came back negative, it turns out she is allergic to the new brand of douche she had used, the doctor said to use real vinegar, and white soap, no more Caress or Summer's Eve for her, time for change!

Dr. Robert Schuller Quotes
-if you listen to your fears, you will never know what a great person you might have been.
-Every achiever that I have ever met says my life turned around when I began to believe in me.

-better to do something imperfectly, than to do nothing flawlessly.
-What great things would you attempt, if you knew you could not fail?

Lou Holtz Quotes
- Ability is what you're capable of doing, motivation determines what you do, attitude determines how well you do it.
- You are bored with life, if you don't get up every morning with a burning desire to do things, you don't have enough goals
- Never tell your problems to anyone, 20% don't care, and the other 80% are glad you have them
- It's not the load that breaks you down, it's the way you carry it.
- Don't tell me how rocky the sea is, just bring the ship in.

Strick fear, or get struck- Nike

Worship God in spirit and in truth, it is always a good thing to separate yourself and spend time with God, it replenishes me, gives me hope, and energy.

9/25/15

"Tyrese and I are still going through our ups and downs, one minute we are arguing, the next we are fucking, it is a vicious cycle, but I still love him, because we do have our moments. I just want him to love me, and to give me his all, I am going to stop giving so much of me to him".

10/8/15

Kelli still has been talking to Tyrese, but not as much, they do not fuck as much either, it was only five times last month, twice in one day, none yet for this month, but she is cool with that. Kelli is able to take time and get his dick off her brain, now she can focus more on herself. She says that she is done with sex, and him.

12/5/15

"Tyrese called me last Friday out of the blue and said that he was on his way to my house, to pick me up". "What is he on?" Kelli thought. "He says that he misses me, I and was missing him too. I had not even made it home yet from work, and he was pulling, just as I was. I took off my scrub top in the driveway and put on a cute little jacket I had on the passenger's side of my car, then got in the car with him. We went riding, talking, listening to music, and made a few stops, on the last stop, he is getting me a bottle of patron, and he sees some of his homies. They are talking about a party going down right now across the street at the club. He gets back in the car, and says we going to the party. I am arguing with him, because although I looked cute, I did not to wear what I had on, he said, "you look good baby, motherfuckers gone look either way, but you with me, who you trying to impress, I say you look good". I felt cute, "I was like okay baby let's go, hell I already got who I want". He paid entrance fees, and we were in. It was cool, not packed, plenty of standing room, I saw some folks I knew, we spoke, and kept it moving. Tyrese introduced me to his people as his girl, I was shocked, "who he is flexing for", is all I could think. He had been spending money and flexing since he picked me up.

but I did not care, I liked it, he really did miss me. He asked me if he could give a female friend of his a hug, he is in my earing explaining, I was like ok, and he tried to get me to jump in a picture with the group, I should have, but that was not his picture, and I did not know them, they do not need a picture of me, just keep my drinks coming, and keep the music going, since I did not get a chance to drink my patron. We left the club after about an hour, and went to his friend's house, where the after party was going down. I had never been to this friend's house before. I was standing with my back up against the wall, listening to this girl talk about something, then I looked up and saw this fine ass tall chocolate man, he caught my attention, his build, the way he was just focusing on his shit, I could not take my eyes off him, even when he felt me staring and our eyes locked, I could not blink, I could not turn my head, I smiled, he smiled back, I smiled at him a few more times, only to see him smiling back. Tyrese came out of nowhere, put his arm around me and said "it is time to go baby", as he kissed me, he had just been showing out in front of everyone. "Why you do not do that shit when it is just us?" But anyway, I liked it. I liked ole dude too, I have to find out who he is, they say his name is Huncho, I like that. I hit up a few connects, the next day, and one slid him my number. I was excited when he called the day after I sent for him. He was charming, and I wanted him, he looks like he knows exactly what to do. The first time I went to go see him, we talked and laughed a bit, he told me that he and Tyrese went to high school together, that they were cool, but not friends, not that I cared, I love Tyrese, but he plays with my heart,

I wanted revenge! Huncho and I came to an understanding of what was going down, after riding around all night, we went back to my place, and it was amazing, he did everything I wanted, exactly how I wanted it, he did it so good, it was so big, I could not even get up there and ride it how I wanted, after talking all that shit, listening to K. Michelle's songs, "cry" and "something about the night", I could not take it, he was solid. I liked it, all this week we have been seeing each other, he even offered to go to the laundromat with me one night, I thought this was a bit weird, but I did not care, I wanted to see him. It was not packed in the laundry room, and I started to fuck him, right there on the chair. We were rubbing and kissing all over each other, I was grinding on him, while he grabbed on my booty, and then titties, he was grinding back, I bounced on him, I felt him rising, I was wet, I had to get up off him, because people so fucking nosey just kept watching, I will finish him off when we get back to my place, and I did just that. The next night, I went to see him again, we fucked right there in the drive way, it was so good, we fucked for two hours. That was our fucking spot two nights in a row, the last day he said somebody heard and probably saw us. So today we came to my house again, he is so fine, and the sex is so good, I made him breakfast, he said that it looked like something they tried to serve him in jail, and that he was not really hungry, we laughed all morning about that, I called him a little later after he left this morning, to let him know that this has to stop, he thought that I was afraid of Tyrese finding out, but I told him that it was just fun, and he said that is was the same for him too, and that he understood. I told him I loved him, he said he loves me too, and we parted ways, but I will never forget how good it was, and how well he follows directions, and how he really did not need directions, but my heart was somewhere else."

1/28/16

"Well, well, well, what do we have here trying to creep upon me, stress, and depression, but blessings outweighing it all. Trying to get over him, I choose to carry the burden. I know that everything is going to be just fine and fall into place at the right time, because God is good.

I really want to write and tell my story, I want to write the negative, tell my problems, but I also want to write about the positive, and all my blessings. It is a new year, and I am still sleeping with Tyrese, but why?"

Kelli just wants to be in love, and be loved in return! Life

2/1/16

"Here is what I had a dream about, a girl and a guy are friends with benefits, they talk every day, text, send selfies, fuck unprotected, she is on depo birth control shot, and he is happy that she lets him cum in her sometimes, they kiss, hug, and keep each other's secrets, they drink, Hennessy for him, patron for her, and she smokes marijuana, no cigs my nig, or anything else, he does not smoke. They tell each other they love each other. She thought they were basically best friends, this had been going on for almost a year now, but after around nine months in to it, she began to fall in love with him. Now, in the beginning when they first started talking, there was a mutual understanding that they were friends, and that they will see where it goes. They even still saw other people, but her feelings towards him started to show, and as he begins to recognize that she no longer just loves him as a friend, and that she is in love with him, and wants only him, and for him to have only her, but he is not ready for that. He like things how they are, but as time goes on, the talking on the phone every day, sending selfies, and hanging out started to slow down. They would still fuck often. One day after having the best sex they agreed they ever had together, since they both had quite a long orgasm. He began to tell her that he knows that she is deeply in love with him, and that they had to slow down, or stop all together, so that her feelings would not get hurt, but her feelings were already hurt, she was so very deeply in love with him, she could not figure out why she loved him so much, and with so much of her heart. The love she had for him, she is glad that she did not give her all because it was a friend fuckship, kind of relationship anyway. He says he had been waiting at least two months to tell her this now, she was surprised that after this long he wanted to break it off basically, seeing that she had caught feelings, but the news she had for him was going to be shocking to him, just as the news he had delivered, was heart stopping to her. She missed a depo shot, and is six, almost seven weeks pregnant, and thought it was going to be good, but after hearing what he just said, she was skeptical about telling him, because she knows that he might think she is trying to set him up, but hopefully, he would not be stupid enough to think that, because he got her pregnant seven weeks ago, and this just happened, but anyway, she chooses not to tell him right then. As she walks around in her bedroom, while he gathered his things, he says to her, "and I know you are pregnant"! Shocked! She sits down on the bed and ask him, "how did you know", and that she was just debating if now was a good time to say anything or not, "he responds, "yea, now is perfect, may be the last time you ever see me anyway". She has never seen him so furious, and upset, frustrated, and angry. Her threw her some money, here is $800, get an abortion, and lose my number, then slams her door as he exits her home. She is all cried out, and with children already, she could not bear to have another child, no dad, no husband, so she calls planned parenthood, and schedules an appointment. She informs him of the appointment through text and lets him know that she will need a driver. As she is in the back at her appointment, he is not allowed back there, all you could hear was her crying, other patients are looking around, for the noise. He started to feel sad to ask her to have this done, because he does love her, he is afraid of being hurt again by a woman who he trusts and cares for. After twenty minutes or so, she comes from the back, head down, jacket zipped, hood on, papers in hand, and begins walking towards the door, he gets up to follow. As they are sitting in the car, he touches her hair, and then her thigh, and expresses how sorry he is, that she had to go through that pain, and that he had heard her screaming and crying. Then she simply hands him a sheet of paper with an ultrasound stapled to it. The papers explain the ultrasound results and has her information on it. As he begins to read, "we regret to inform you that an abortion could not be done today, because you are having twins, so the price doubled, plus there is a $20 charge for each week occurring during the pregnancy", and on top of that, it read, "you are already ten weeks pregnant, so if you can come up with that amount by next Thursday, since we are booked next Friday, we can go ahead and schedule the procedure". He looks at her and says twins, she looks at him and starts crying again, this time putting her head closest to her lap, as he drives off. When they arrive to her home, he volunteered to help her into the house, so they go in. She sits on the sofa, with sad and hurt written all over her face. He walks into the living room, after locking the door. She asks him, "so what's next?" He walks up to where she is sitting and begins to choke her, saying "bitch Ima beat them out of you, that is what's next! She is punching and pushing to get him off her, he gets up, and slaps her so fucking hard in her face, it left his hand print, then he punches her, she falls to the floor, he kicked her in her belly, or so he thought, she was protecting it, by holding it. He punches her at least eight times, until she let out a cry so loud, he had never heard before, and stepped back, he looked around confused, and angered, he grabbed his keys and ran out the door. She laid there another hour, cried half the time, and thought to herself, "I really have to get an extra $800, within seven days". He really took all his anger out on her, whatever he is upset about, he showed it when he beat her up, He whopped her ass so bad, when she woke up, she did not know she was in the hospital, nor how she got there. She did not recall all that had happened, she did not know that she ended up sleeping on the floor, all beat up, nose bloody, and tears, it was the middle of the day, she was supposed to get her children from school. She never showed up, so her sister went to get them, and bring them home, since she has an extra key, the oldest child called the aunt, when he did not see his mom, and when his mom did not answer the phone, or return his call. Her sister walks into her house first, then turns the corner to see her sister laying there, not knowing if she was dead or alive. She dialed 911, and checked for a pulse, at the same time. She feels a very faint pulse, and begin to cry, the kids begin to cryas well, as the paramedics arrive, everyone is still crying and calling family. She is alive one said, they took her to the hospital, and when she woke up, she looked around and there were some family members, police detectives, security, and she is panicking!

"How did I go from sleeping on the floor, to waking up in a hospital, and why do I not remember the trip here" she thought. She was confused and hurt. The nurse, who is standing by her, taking her vital signs, ask her if she knows where she was. She replies "yes, a hospital". A police detective asked if she had known her attacker, "no", she replied, as the nurse finishes, her family members walk over one bends down, and asked if it was the guy that she was pregnant by, "Now, how did she know I was pregnant?" The nurse had informed her family, while she was passed out, that the babies were okay as poor nurse, she felt bad, and was just as shocked as they were, to find out, that her family did not yet know. So, they kept her in the hospital to monitor her and the babies overnight. She learned that she had fell and hit her head, after trying to stand after such a brutal beating, but they wanted to know about the black eyes, and busted lip. She told the detectives again, that she knew nothing, so that they would leave, pretending she could not reach, forcing one to leave his card down somewhere, asking her to call, if she remembers anything at all. She slept like a baby that night, soaking up all the rest she could get, knowing that come morning, after breakfast she would be discharged. Her mother came to pick her up from the hospital, takes her to get prenatal vitamins filled, and home, where her sister is, with her children, who are playing on their phones and tablets, and with their dolls, race cars, and each other, getting alone. Her house is clean, her sister baked pizza, and even made up the bed with extra pillows on it. She thanks her mom and sister, as they leave out the door, blowing kisses, and catching them as they blow them back. She waits until everyone is in their cars, before closing and locking the door. She goes into the living room with her kids, and asks how they been, and that she misses and loves them, even though it was one night. They were also wondering, who did it, and everyone else already had their minds made up. She told her kids that she did not see the person, as much as she wanted to be honest, she still was in love with him, and that is why she is protecting him. As the day settled down, they ate dinner, and she put her kids to bed, after their baths. As she got out the shower, body dripping wet, she put on her t-shirt and panties, her phone had been on the charger since she got home, thanks to her sister. She picked it up off the charger, 100% full battery, she powered it on, and there were 15 voice messages (the max; it is full), and seven text messages, that was a lot for her. One text from her mom, one text from her sister, and five from him, begging her to pick up, and not to tell the police anything, that he is sorry, and that he loves her. After deleting the texts, she checked the voicemail. 14 out of 15 messages are from him, half of them not saying anything, but on one of them he was crying. She hangs up the phone, wanting to call him, but she did not, instead, she got in the bed, prayed, and went to sleep, after putting her phone on silent. No work in the morning for her, and no school for the kids, because the weekend had arrived. As morning arose, things are looking good, kids are up, eating cereal, and watching cartoons. Good morning, I love you, she says to her children, as she is walking into the living room, and then goes to make a bowl of cereal for herself, but the doorbell rings, her heart started to pound faster as she is walking closer to the door, only for it to be him. The kids are happy to see him, because she had told them that he killed the person that did that to her, so there was no need to mention it again, or to believe what everyone else says. He speaks to the kids, and gives them hugs and bags of goodies, they go upstairs into her room, he has a big bag for her as well, but she wanted to hear him out, and he began to talk, telling her that he was so sorry, and that he was surprised and disappointed that he hit a woman, and that he has not hit a woman since elementary school. He apologized over and over, begging her to forgive him, he exclaims that he really does love her, and wants to not only see her happy, but be that person to make her happy, and that he wanted to marry her, and was prepared to ask at that moment. He is there crying out to her that he loves her, and has been unable to eat, drink, sleep, work right, think right, and that he needs her, or else there is no point in living. She tells him that he will never hit her again, not even playing, and demands respect. Trust is good, she trusted him, and he trusts her, but she wanted more communication between them, that they communicate every day, to make sure there is a clear understanding of everything. She wants loyalty, and for him to never leave her alone to raise their children, by the way she has four, and he has three, and she is pregnant with two, that is nine kids, and if married, he will continue to help take care of their kids and do more things together as a family. They kissed and made up within a short few hours. He had plans for the two of them (ring in pocket) to go out and have a romantic night, he told her that they were going out to eat, "yea, okay", she told him. After he left, she went back to continue making her cereal, her children where fine, she sat next to one and watched cartoons, after that episode, she went to get dressed, and so did the kids. They played games, puzzles, cards, tea cups, and race car tracks. She stood there smiling, while making lunch, watching her children play together, and get alone. After that long day, she put her kids to bed, climbed in bed herself, turned on a movie, and finally decided to text him back. He had been calling and texting all day since he left, and she did not completely ignore him, she had replied to a text earlier, but it was in between games with her kids, anyway, she wanted to be held, and knew just who wanted to hold her, and her small, but growing belly, with twins inside, she hopes that they are boys, her son needs a brother. He came over, showered, and slide directly behind her, holding her with the perfect grip, rubbing her belly, and her left side, since she is laying on her right. He is tongue kissing her shoulder and her neck. He turns her head with two fingers towards him, she turns, and he moves as close as she could, as they begin to kiss so passionately. He takes off her shirt, and starts sucking, and caressing and stroking her breast, his hands were so firm, but he was gentle with her. He kissed her body down to her panties, where he removed them with his mouth. He is licking and sucking her pussy until she comes, then he climbs on top, after a while, she turns to her side, and he fits himself into her, pounding, and stroking, pushing deep, kissing and caressing her. He made her come so many times the bed was soaked, and he came twice. He is making love to her, then he holds her all night as they fell asleep, both satisfied, and in love. They woke up, showered, and went to Denny's, she went back home, and he left out for work, he had his own businesses, a car wash, and a barber shop. Later that night, when he returned, the kids were asleep. He brushed up against her from behind, gripping her sides, just the way she liked it. He wraps his arms around her waist while kissing her neck, then starts caressing her sweet breasts, as she stands towards the stove cooking, she turned the skillet off just in time, he picked her up, and laid her gently on the kitchen table, staring deeply into her eyes. In he went, loving the sounds she made, as she controlled his entrance, and she loved that he loved it. Kissing on her breast, and deep stroking her made her come quick, which only made him go even harder, saying "aaaw shit baby, I feel you coming, mmmhm, get yours, that's one", she is moaning, and pulling him deeper, one arm by his waist, and one around his back, legs wrapped in a baby making lock, lol, if you know what that is, he picks her up, still stroking, feeling her stroke back, he laid her on the floor next to the stove, and fucked her so good. Slow fucking, fast fucking, when he goes deep, she grips as tight as she can, he won, she started crying, but only a few tears dropped, because on that last stroke, he knows he went extra hard, she tried her best to hold on, but it is what it is, he was the man, her man. D game on point, back to it he turned her around onto a chair, and slid on in, pounding, holding her hips, grabbing her hair, moaning and trying to keep balance, while she throws it back. He caught it too, and she was stuck right there, he hit that spot, she came, shaking like she was having convulsions, legs vibrating at the speed of light, well at least she felt that way. He came all inside her, then she turned and sat him on the chair, and stuck his half hard back inside of her, and started tongue kissing him, rolling her hips, and vibrating on it, while he gets the rest of his nut out. She kissed his neck, and chest, then his ear and started to bounce a little, she got wetter and wetter, he moaned as he continued to come. They tongue kissed so passionately, for so long. She finally got off him, I love you she says, I love you too baby he replied. "Can you run the shower" she asked. "Anything for you" he said, she went into the living room, and laid across the couch, then they showered, here he goes again, he loved the smell of her fresh pussy. The very moment she dropped the towel, he walks up to her and picks her up, and starts to eat her pussy, while walking towards the bed, he lay her down, kiss her lips and tells her he loves her. They both just lay there, still hungry, but fall asleep. Then she woke up only to realize that it was all a dream, everything.

2/2/16

Kelli just wants to work for herself and have a man she can call hers. She wants to ride so bad, and Tyrese, who she is back fucking is starting to get old, she was a freak, and liked trying new things, she even taught him a new sex position, that she had learned from Grimms. She really wants to be over Tyrese already, but something is keeping her from moving on away from him. She figures she needs to change her focus, but she is unable to focus on what she wants to focus on. She needs to stop letting him fuck her like he is her man, because she gets deeper into her feelings, even though her mind says no, her heart, and her body says yes. "Why?", she cries out. There are so many things she wants to do, and so many dreams she wants to accomplish, it is difficult for her to stay focused on a certain one, especially, when she has to play the waiting game, on getting this business structured, so she starts a new project, only having to stop it, and go back to the first one, once the wait is over. Plus, that dream felt so real, it scared her. "Someone told me my red wine looks poisonous, like that red apple that Eve bit, while in the garden", "I cannot believe you put that poison in your body" is what was said. "That is deep. Hell, I am poisoning my body, and it is sad. I do not understand why I continue to do it. I keep trying to cry, but it will not come out, and I have been having the craziest dreams lately. Why can I not be great? Why do I feel like this, helpless, and hopeless? I know that God is taking care of me, why must I constantly tempt him? He is always good, and whatever the devil has, God has better. Stop slipping and stop tripping over things that do not exist. Old ass feelings that you know are gone. When will you realize? When will you act? I am tired of you already, get it together, we all fall down, you need to get up, got your head hung low". Nothing seemed to be working, but then again, she has not been giving it her all. Oh lord, be with her.

2/12/16

"I will sometimes just sit and ponder of how things may not work, if I try them, I should stop that", Kelli writes.

"My heart is so not as open as it used to be, I guess it comes from praying to God to make me cold hearted. I feel it has come true."

Kelli does not feel the same about Tyrese anymore, she cares about him, but that is it. She does not feel that he cares for her. They had sex again last night, why will they not just leave each other alone. It has been over ten months now, and she treats him just like he treats her. This guy is so crazy, he acts like he does not care, now she does the same. If he gets disrespectful, she does as well, he does not like that. And now, after sex when he tries to talk and sit around, she hands him his shit and tells him he needs to go. He looked so surprised, but happy still. He gave her a rather nice hug at the door, and no kissing now. In the beginning he used to beg her for a kiss. He would kiss all over her body, from her neck to her pretty pussy. His head was not the best, but she missed it. He said to her that doing things like that gets people in their feelings, and that he thinks she is in love, head over heels for him. He asks her often, and again last night, "Do you love me? Just be honest, I know you in love with me''. "No, I am not" she said. She thinks to herself "I cannot fall in love with him, he is full of shit, I just like his sex, and his chest". He hates when she rides, he says it make him cum faster, but she is thinking, "that is because I do my thang and puts it down, last night Kelli got on top, and rode for maybe one minute, Tyrese was moaning and came all in her again, of course she was pissed, got that dick back hard and bent over for him, she wanted her nut too, and she got two of them, she slept great last night. But those feelings of her wanting to be in love are not for him anymore, he needed to get his attitude together, and show her that he cares, if he does.

2/16/16

"I feel like that Jamie Fox song, "I always fall for your type", I swear I always fall for the same type of men. WTF? I still believe in love though, unlike half the world I see yelling fuck love. No, fucking love those who love you! If you know and feel that they do not love you, then fuck them. When I see that, I believe they are not speaking of real love. With so many things going on in my mind, it is a bit difficult to focus on one thing at a time, I must multi-task, to make myself feel useful, or feel like I am doing something to move closer toward each goal".

2/16/16

"Communication is key. He wants to be more open to communicating, but most men do not want to talk about their problems unless they feel as though they can handle it, then they start talking about how they are going to solve them. Tyrese was not upset while they were talking about it. Kelli is just happy that he is talking about it, but she knows that there is something else he is not ready or willing to discuss, so she left it on him, for when is ready on his own terms. She just listened. She now knows that he does wants to be with her but is afraid of getting his feelings crushed, he keeps reminding her of this, but she is afraid of the same thing, plus being used by someone, but she is brave enough to keep trying. They have been on a roller coaster ride since what feels like forever. He told her that he does not trust her, yet he continues to come around and even ask to bring his child from time to time. How dare you leave your child with a person you say you do not trust. Where are you going and what are you doing so important? Even if it is only for a few hours or so, I wish I would leave mine with someone I do not trust, my child, child please!"

3/2/16

"I cannot and will not continue to be used, and neglected, treated like a hair ball being pushed under a rug. I will not lower my standards for your acceptance, if anything I can upgrade you. I will continue to walk with my head held high because I know that regardless of any situation, problem, trail, road block, or person that tries to tear me down, I will be alright because God got me. My hero, my Lord, my Savior will not let me fall without bouncing back even better.

I will have self- control. I will take care of myself and my children always. I will not be sold a dream, men will not be my weakness, I will no longer seek them. I have found a great strength within me, and slowly as I go through tribulations, my strength grows. I am now stronger and happier with where I am in life right now. I am thankful, grateful, and give all praise to God, because without him, there is no me."

"I will stop acting so desperate for a man, trying to play their games, and getting my feelings hurt. I just want a real for real, no cheating, in love type of relationship with a man who is respectful, responsible, dependable (although I am an independent woman), someone who does not mind cuddling, and listening, a mutual understanding, become my best friend, my homie lover friend. I will ride his ass crazy and suck him like a lollipop! "

Try to keep it PG rated, "I write what I want, this is my story"!

Well, okay then!

3/2/16

"I cannot believe that I waited for him to come." "I started to text him and say, "your words no longer hold value to me, unless followed by immediate action. I have never chased anyone, male or female, to be my friend, but I do expect people to keep their word, because your word is your bond, it is how your trust is gained, it shows your loyalty, and honesty, and dependability, keeping your word is valuable, I understand that there are things that may come up, where you are unable to keep a commitment, but out of caring, and respect of the other person's time, communicate with them, via text, call, or whatever, to inform them of a need to reschedule, even if you have to call back at a later time to do so, not ignore them", "but I did not press send". Scared of what? For what?

"Even pass my own thought and beliefs, there is a higher power, that will help me to change my life around, and live the life that I am willing to work for".

3/6/16

Kelli decided to go out last night, she put on her little sexy black dress, and four-inch sexy black heels, she had her jewelry on, and her clutch in her hand, she was looking good and feeling good. She stopped to get herself a few drinks at a few different bars, it was cold out, but the liquor and moving around helped, she went downtown to the casino, to win some money. She was really feeling herself, plus Tyrese was blowing up her phone, she answered it, once she was downtown. What a coincidence, he was downtown at the casino as well, as soon as she gets out the car, he hops out of the car with his friend, and walks up to her. "What do you think you doing, don't get fucked up tonight", he said. "She laughed, because that meant she was looking good, she gave him a hug, and they started walking. He is so funny, cracking jokes on people as they walk by, this one girl tries to touch him, Kelli's reflexes instantly moved her hand, "do not touch my man" Kelli said. The girl said, "oh, I am sorry, I am a friendly person, I like his necklace", Kelli replied, "I do not care, do not touch him". Her and her friends kept it moving, he laughing, feeling himself, he says, "aw, my baby protective, I did not know you had me like that". Kelli laughs, then says, "yea, okay whatever, you did not stop her from trying to touch your necklace". He said, "because I knew you had me baby", walking up on her, she laughed, and says whatever, he gives her a nice booty rubbing hug, and a few kisses, he was really on her. They continued inside, and made it to the tables, they had a good time, drinking, talking shit, and cashing out. He would kiss her for good luck each new round they played, people kept saying how good they looked together, and Kelli agreed, plus she was loving how he kept kissing on her, and they were winning. It was time to go, and she already knew he was going home with her that night, and he did. He just left, and she enjoyed his company.

3/8/16

Kelli and Tyrese have been hanging out tough, for the last three days, she feels they are closer than ever, after he made up big time for standing her up six days ago. She still loved him, and he knew it, they have slowed down on fucking again, they had sex two days ago, and she told him she loved him, while they were fucking, but he keeps reminding her that they are just going to be friends, and no more fucking, they say, although he tried to fuck yesterday. She almost gave in, they kissed, and she moaned before he even touched her, then he bagged back, and said, "nah, I am not going to do you like that, you might get in your feelings", he was right, but she did not care, she was already in her feelings, and she wanted him, "we are just friends remember, no more sex", she said. They left her place, and rode around that day, while parked waiting on their food, he said that he had a confession. He turned to her, told her that he loved her, but that he was still in love with his baby's mother, and that if she would take him back, that is where he would go, on top of that he asked Kelli if he could use her social media account to contact his baby's mother because she had him blocked, he explained that she was due to have his son, and that he wanted to be there, he expressed that he loved and missed her. "Wow"! Kelli tried her best to keep her cool, "sure, you can use my social media account to try and contact her", those words stung Kelli's throat, as she barely got them out, without crying. She loved him so much, that she did not care that he had just told her that he has a baby on the way, with the woman he loves, and wanted to be with, and that he wanted Kelli to log in her social media account, to help reconnect them. Kelli simply wants to do anything to make him happy, and to be there as a friend, silly girl, her heart was broken, but she could not see him like that, he was desperate, that is how she wanted him to feel about her, she wishes that she was the one having his baby, and the one that he wanted to be with, but she was not. "Maybe he is just fucking with me, she thought, "but no, I do not know". She gave him access, he had her phone, and took it inside with him to get the food. "I just hope that he put his number in her messages and asked that she call, I hope he did not say anything that required a response, hopefully he sent one long ass detailed message, so that the girl will know that it is him, and that she did not to need to reply, but to text or call him instead", Kelli thought to herself. He was coming back to the car, still texting. "See", Kelli said, as she turned to get her phone that he was handing back to her, along with the food they were waiting for. "I am being a good friend, I let you use my phone", they laughed and went on about their day, she did not believe that sent his baby's mother a message, although he said he did, but if so, he must have deleted it. Night came, and they were still out riding the streets, after being together all day. Tyrese wanted some head, and Kelli gave it to him, while he was driving, he loved it, and he almost crashed the car trying to fight it. Once she was done, they kissed, continued to ride and listen to Future. Everyone was getting ready to go their separate ways, after hanging around. Tyrese told his friends that he would meet up with them later. Kelli had been drinking heavy, ever since he gave his confessions, she wanted to fuck him in the car, but she made him spill his drink, when she hoped on him while he was driving. He pulled over for her, she climbed on him, but they both could not fit behind the steering wheel, without him letting the seat back, he tried, but got angry because she was rushing, and pushed her off him, her reflexes hit him, with a quick two piece, Bing bow! Then he slapped her and she started crying, he said, "bitch is you crazy, do not ever put your hands on me," she hit him again and said, "you hit me too, you should not have pushed me off you", they sat there arguing loud, back and forth, as people watch, he called his friend, and got in the car with him, she drove off, and went home. When she got home she checked all her messages from social media, his baby's mother had replied saying 'who is this', so Kelli told her who she was, and that her baby's daddy was not shit, and that he hit her, Kelli lied and told her that she was pregnant by him too, but getting an abortion, his baby's

mother replied, " do not ever let a man push you to where you will go and kill your baby". That was some real shit! Kelli replied, "fuck him, fuck that, and good luck with him". Kelli did not wait for a reply, she instantly blocked the girl, and him too, just in case he tried to send a message. Kelli had also blocked him from her phone. He called the next morning from a different number, threatening to kill Kelli and her children, saying that she is trying to ruin "their" relationship. "Nigga first of all, your baby's mother does not want you, and I am not trying to ruin anything, fuck you", Kelli said. "Yes, you are bitch", he said, "you just mad because I want her and not you, you mad because I love her, and I do not love you". Those words pierced her heart, it was true, she hung up on him. He called right back, "yea, bitch, why did you tell her you was pregnant by me, you did not want a baby, when I tried to get you pregnant, bitch, fuck you, you will never have my baby", he said. "Fuck you bitch, stop calling my phone, it is over with now, so bye!" she said, and she hangs up again. He called back, he says, in a tone that she had never heard before, and she has heard rage out of him before, "Bitch I will pull up right now, and shoot that motherfucker up, now keep playing with me, do not tell my baby's mother shit, I will kill you bitch, I am right around the corner, you think I am playing with you, on my kids, I will pull up at your crib, and your mother's crib, I have never fucked with you". Kelli was scared shitless, she believed him, she woke her kids up, and hurried quickly to go warn her family, no one was there, but her younger brother. She called her other brother, and told him what was up, and asked for a gun, or for him to come through, he said no, and hung up. She went to the pawn shop to buy a gun, but they would not let her get it the same day, due to some process. Kelli could not wait! She knew where her brothers kept their guns, but they did not want to give her one so, she chose one on her own, there were several to choose from. She had already applied for her license to carry, and knew how to use the gun she chose, plus she went to the shooting range a few times, with that same type of gun, so she is feeling confident. She warned her younger brother who was there, he said okay. She called around, no action from anyone. She goes to drop her kids off, to a secured location. Tyrese calls her again, saying "I see you not at home right now", she hangs up, then go down to the police station to make a report, because she felt threatened for her life, she is crying hysterically, they tell her to calm down, and also told her that next time she comes up to a jail, not to come smelling like weed, but she did not care, because her life and her family's life was at risk, and she needed to take action. They filed the report, even pulled his background up, it was way more extensive than what she had found online, "Geesh, how did you end up with a guy like this, he has a long rap sheet, including battery and assault", the officer said, while shaking his head at her. "Was he your weed man", another officer asked. "No, now can you just help me, and tell me what I need to do", Kelli said. They informed her that she should go downtown and file a temporary protection order against him, so that if he contacts her again, that he will be arrested. She drove downtown, giving herself time to calm down from her panic attack, he texted her while she is driving, he says, "yea, bitch, you think I am playing, you keep texting my baby's mother", at this point he is delusional, because she, had been blocked the both of them, but he keeps texting from a different number. He continues, "I just left your mother's crib, and your brothers know what is up. Kelli never responded to any of the text, and blocked that number as soon as she parked. She ran into the court building, heart racing, she filed for the temporary protection order, it was granted, and she was given some papers. She felt as though she had done her part, she warned everyone, she filed a report, she got an order of protection, and she had a gun, that she was not afraid to use if she had to, but she was hoping that she did not have too. She was now afraid of the man she was just loving on, and who she thought she was is in love with. She went back to her house, and packed some clothes, and other essentials. She is paranoid, and is constantly looking out the window, and she was shocked when she saw him driving slowly down her street, he saw her car, but kept going, thank God. She was afraid, but, she was strapped, and her children were safe, and she was not too afraid to defend herself. Just to have it on record, she called the police officer who filed the report, and told him that she had just seen Tyrese. They came and drove down the street a few times, which helped, she was able to get her things, and she never saw him again. She got a few texts from him, asking her to please answer the phone, so she answered, but he kept with the threats, and shit talking, she asked him, "You really will kill me and my kids?" "Yes, because you should not have lied to my baby's mother". He said. "You lie about shit all the time Tyrese, you lied to her too, about fucking with me", she said. "Bitch, you smashed the homie, yea, you think I did not know about that, bitch, you better not tell my business, I will fuck you up, stay away from my family", he said. "First of all, you talking like

I been knew you had a family, let alone a baby on the way, then you had the nerve to use my page to contact her, when you knew how I felt, fuck you, why fuck with me for so long, if you was going to do me wrong?" she asked. "Yea, you right I do not know why, I fucked with you for so long, I do not know what I was thinking", he said. "Why did you fuck the homie", he asked again, "what was you thinking", he went on, " I hope you did not think it would make me jealous", he said. "I did not fuck him" she replied, but she was lying, they both knew the truth, but fuck that, she was not going to admit it, and she did not. He hung up on her, after he cursed her out a few more times. She did not care, she was hurting, she could not stop crying.

3/9/16

Kelli is back home, she thinks she saw his car parked down the street from her house, he did say that he was fucking with someone who lived over there, the first day he had ever came to her house. She was not taking any chances, if she wanted to change her life and get back on the right track she must move, so she started to sell everything in her house, "fuck everybody", she said, they all gone miss me. She called him twice, just to make sure he was not still tripping, because she was still shook, and he still knew her whereabouts, and her schedule, she listened to the background, and then hang up, as long as she did not hear any wind, she felt as though he was sitting still somewhere, and that she was not being watched, but her heart was still broken, she just knew that he was going to show up at any time, to end her and her kids lives. She decided two days ago that she was moving, and now she has posted everything for sale. She had a nice house, full of everything one needs, with nice furniture, that sold quickly. She was racking her money up, from her furniture, and doing hair. She lost her job when she got depressed, but still was going to school.

3/13/16

Kelli had been planning her move since the seventh, everything was now set. She had found a place to live, she found new schools, and doctors for her and her kids, she mapped out the grocery stores, the parks, and the local library. She had plans on what she would do, everything is packed in the car, her house was now empty, and she was ready to go. She was leaving in the morning, to move out of state. She was hurting, and needed to get away to clear her mind, and focus on something better, her papers had come through for her new business, and she has to move it, right when it was getting started.

3/15/16

She is in her new place now, she is so sad and depressed, she misses him so much, she loved him, "how could I have been so blind?", she wonders. All she does is cry and drink, even started back smoking. She was looking on her social media account, where her brother posted that he hopes ole dude finds her and kills her, before he does, he even mentioned her location and said that she needed to bring his gun back. She felt bad about taking his gun, but as much shit as she does for him, and her family, most of them owed her money, and he owed her more than what the gun is worth. Kelli never responded, her heart was heavy, now her favorite brother wants her dead too, this is crazy, it is too much to handle right now.

6/17/16

I do not understand how some women will allow men to live with them, and he does not do anything for you. He does not pay bills, put food on the table, and he is disrespectful, why is he still there? He treats you like dog shit, and yet you continue to allow these things to go on. I have been in a situation where a man tried to live off me, but that first time he refused to pay a bill, and I knew he had the funds, I kicked him straight out, go back with your mama's, and live for free, because it is not going down like that here. I cut that shit short quick, the sex was good, but it could not pay for anything.

"Girl, mind your business"! "But she came and told me this, I do not want to hold it in, hell I got my own issues, I am letting out, the fuck I want to hold hers for, do not tell me shit.

9/11/16

"You move mountains, you cause walls to fall, with your power, perform miracles. There is nothing that's impossible and we're standing here only because you made a way! (one of my favorite songs by Travis Greene) Thank you Lord. I cannot thank you enough. It is time I step up and face my fears Lord I need you to help me Lord! Kelli screams. You said to lean totally upon you Lord and rely on no one else Lord. So, I put all my trust and faith into you Lord!

I give you all of me Lord. I am sick Lord, sick of the pattern that I am going in. I want to follow you Lord, I need to, it is the only way Lord, and it is the way I want to go Lord. Come rescue me! I need to spend more time with you so that when I draw closer to you Lord you will draw closer to me, my God. When I spend more time with you Lord, it makes me feel so special Lord and loved. I have peace thanks to you Lord. I want that again, to be at peace, at peace with my mind, since my mind controls my actions. The negative things I think, I should not say, so I stopped speaking on them a little because I still do it often and do not speak on the good thoughts as I should. I can just say them out loud to myself. I must learn to reject negative thoughts as soon as they come and do not give in to them. Do not self-destruct! I will not be defeated because God is with me even right now. I must give more to try and quit smoking, my God you have done it before you can do it again. And this time I must do my part consistently and not give up nor give in. I have to go all the way through this time. I will not and cannot give up. I must go on, change is hard, but God will help me and carry me through my mess. He will lift me up and I will stand above all the difficulties and test that come my way, each and every day. I will handle them with God by my side, I will conquer my fears, I will not be defeated, I will not back down, I will stand, I will enjoy my life, I will not allow my problems to overcome me, I will overcome! I will stop thinking, "oh no you cannot", because oh yes I can! Because when God says yes who am I to say no. I want what He wants for me above all that I want or think. He is the Almighty. His thoughts are higher than mine, what He thinks of me is way higher than what I think of myself. I must follow through and be courageous. I must stop stressing and worrying, it is doing me no good. Just put your trust and faith in God that He will continue to make a way for you, and know that He is love. I must grow and change and be free from these foolish things I allow to control me. I need to free my mind, make it up, keep it set and follow it. Stick to what I say that I will do. You are your most valuable commodity, learn to love and appreciate yourself, you are a good person God will always love you for who you are because he made you. Be true to yourself, work smarter, do better with your health, children, finances, education, and be wise in all your ways, God said so! Be not deceived by your heart, conquer your fears, so what, forget about what people say, that is their problem. Do what is best for you and your children".

12/15/16

Feeling freaky, I just want to have an orgasm, a hard long one, where not only my legs are shaking but my entire body is trembling. I want to feel that constant flow of my juices coming on his big hard dick, my pussy throbbing, pulsating, gripping him, as I pull him deeper in me, I am going to lose it, thanks Kegel exercises. Then I want to ride after I wake up from that knockout! I wanted it to happen with who I was dreaming about, but when I pull him deep, that is the furthest he can go, some dream, I want somebody who can really beat it, and not just from the back, he must be able to handle me properly at all angles. I want my hair pulled, ass smacked and kissed, my thighs kissed before he eats it, freak nasty shit. Smoke and fuck all night, just one night, it has been nine months. I am not trying to fall for anyone, I do not want that right now, unless he good to me, not cheap, and not afraid to speak his mind, he should be independent, not living with anyone, has his own car and can show me around town, take me shopping and show me how much he wants me, until then I will get what I need and keep it moving. I do not want to be thotty, but if he is not pleasing me, then why stay? No, I am on a mission, and if he cannot give it to me like I want, then he is not for me. He got to go hard, and fuck me good, I want to feel it for weeks. I only want it with one person. I want to make him cum and feel good like how he does me, this is daydreaming, I like it when we are fucking and love to hear him moan when he is about to cum. I want to kiss his neck again, his body, while he is doing his thing, then lay him down and proceed. Man, when I cum, he gone drown, my body ready, adrenaline pumping, blood rushing, heart pacing. What a nice workout, so pleasurable, I am going to be so very committed to this workout, I will not tap out, or give up, or give in. I want it, I will get it. Woooh, Glad that is out of my system.

12/23/16

He will contribute to my smile, I will like him, I will be mentally and sexually attracted to him. His freak must match mine and he must give great massages. Not only that, he must respect that I have children, I want to go deep, I want to be able to stimulate his mind, have fun, enjoy times together with my children and him. He will be so sweet to them and to me, show that he cares, he will say it and show it, in many ways. I want his time, his heart, his attention, his secrets, his trust, his love and understanding, and I want him to give them to me. And vice versa. It will feel good, to be cared about. We will explore new adventures and fantasies.

1/3/17

"My mind is changing, I am not dreaming about sex as much as I used to, I still get horny, but I work out now as a reliever, and take cold showers. I am looking to get a therapist, it has been almost one year, and I still think about Tyrese. Maybe I should fuck somebody else to help get over him, but I cannot deny the fact that I missed him. I loved the way he would make me laugh when we would play around, wrestling or whatever, he would tickle me, and it would be so funny. I loved how he would tell me I looked good, even when I did not feel like I looked good. I have seen him when he was goofy, and playful, when he was serious, when he was hurt, and when he was happy, we bonded in all those moments. I miss his presence, he made me high like no other, just being around him. Or maybe it was all just a play on feelings. I know my feelings were real, because it hurt like hell".

9/25/17

So, you in your feelings now? "No, not really". Kelli writes, "I just want to end things before I get in my feelings. I have learned the hard way already, if you are fucking a guy and you all say that you are just friends, sex must stop with me, because I know that eventually I will catch feelings, and want that person all to myself. Safe sex is good, but protecting my heart is what matters to me, I will not allow me to hurt myself, by continuing in this "fuck friendship" literally, it was good for the two weeks it lasted. So, back to no sex for me, although I still crave him, it will be of no good to me, to go down this path. If I cannot have my way with him like how I want, then he cannot have his way with me like, he wants. I thought Jason would help me to get over Tyrese. It is not right for two friends to be having sex, like we do. Now, do not get me wrong, we do more than just fuck, I like when we talk, mature conversation, we talk about our goals, our problems, try to help each other come up with solutions, hell even a back massage is okay with clothes on, short and sweet. It is the naked massages, and naked sexing that gets me, him kissing me so passionate while we are fucking, putting himself deeper inside of me as I moan and open my legs wider, holding his back as he rocks my body, pleasing me so well. He will put my breasts in his mouth, sucking, as he continues in me, Oh Lord. We turn to the side and my baby still going, and I am still coming, he makes this little moaning sound when I nut on it, which only makes me come harder, then of course he wants it from the back, killing it, all in my guts, and I am loving every second of it, as I grind back and dance on it. But he whispers in my ear, and says he is in control right now, this is his pussy, while pulling my hair and pushing deeper from behind, taking back his control, from me throwing it back. His bed is soaked, I was constantly coming, it was number five for me then, he says, "hold it still right there baby, ooooh yeah, take this big dick baby, ooooh shit", he is loud, beating it, we both moaning, even a little hollering from me. Fuck, we are getting it in hard, like we both got something to get off our chest, "aaw", I came again, this time so did he. "Damn girl, this shit, man!" He exclaims, as he is looking into my eyes, he begins kissing me, and rubbing on my body, "you so soft", he says. He so into me, he strapped up and it was time for round two. Boom, right to kissing my body, then he started to kiss the inside of my thighs, biting them just a tad bit, he is teasing. I knew he was not going all the way down, he says he does not eat pussy (some man you are), but I did not care at that particular moment, I knew from last week that he did not eat pussy, that was fine, I do not suck his dick. Anyways, we are going, I got my legs up, and he has me pinned, I cannot move. "Ooooh shit this some good pussy, ooh shit mm", he comes closer to my face, kisses my neck, and whispers, "ohh yea mmhm", as I moan, "this my pussy, this my pussy, say it, say this my shit", as he goes harder and deeper, I say "yes, baby it is yours", just so he could stop saying that. I want on top now, but he will not let me tonight, "I want to ride baby", "no, I got this right now". Huh, I hate to lay there when I feel like riding, I said to myself, but I am going to let him have his way, right now. He puts me a position I had never been in before, I was amazed. and he handled my body just like a man should, he took his time making sure it felt good to me, he wanted this fuck to last, he kissed the back of my neck and down my spine. While going in nice and slow, it was wet, he grabbed my waist with the perfect grip, and pushed inside me, he rubbed my back, and ass while he was in me. My knees got weak, I had to get off them, so I laid flat on my stomach and omg, this sex was getting to my head, he took it out and eat it from the back, it felt so freaking good, I could not help but to cry out. He put me to sleep, it was so sweet, I felt him wipe me down with a clean warm rag, dried it with another, then laid next to me. I came over and laid on his chest, while he rubbed my side, I rubbed his chest, we talked, and fell asleep. I woke up the next morning, he was already inside of me, oh, it was a wonderful feeling, I love morning sex, it is my favorite, daytime sex period. I did not even try to take control, because I now knew the reason why he wanted control, so, I let him get what he wanted. I was moaning so loud, it felt so good. A tear fell, I was happy that he came quick, that shit was good, I was so wet, and he had done hit the spot, it scared me because that was beyond friendship level and now he done fucked up. I cannot be his friend and come around like shit all cool. "Nah nigga I am going to need for you to be my man if you think we gone keep fucking like this, that shit touched my heart, I cannot be around you, because I am going to touch you, you must think this is a fucking game", is what Kelli told Jason, while he was asking for a kiss and shit, she hesitated, but did not give in, she left and went home. Once Kelli got home, she sat her bag and keys down, then sat on the couch and texted him "I made it home, and you know that really did something to me. The way we have sex, how often we have sex and talk, and chill really got me feeling some type of way forreal. I most certainly understand what you meant last time when you said you cannot see me for at least two months, although you said you were joking, I still agree! I will miss you though, enjoy your day. Jason responds "lol, enjoy your day also". She replies "that is not funny, (so in her feelings), you really make me want you all to myself. I love the way you handle my body, whisper and talk to me when we having sex, how you hold me so tight when I ride it, and even after sex, when you fall asleep on me, when I'm holding you between my legs, and rubbing on your body, I like how we sit and talk about whatever. That shit is amazing. But it is not what friends do. It is all good until feelings get involved". He replies, "well, we might need to slow down… I like our friendship". She replies, "Yea I agree, especially after this morning baby, the sex is going to stop completely, I know how I am and being friends and fucking does not work for me, I tried it too many times and failed. It will be much safer for me and my feelings to just not have sex with you anymore, I do not want to, but I have to, you fuck me like I am yours, and make me say this is yours! You do not belong to me". Kelli responded, she wanted to say, "you will not let me have you like I want you, mentally, emotionally, and sexually", but she said "I mean do not get me wrong, I like for a man to take control, have your fun boo, flip me turn however you want. Get it baby, I love it, it feels great, but when I want to ride, let me, let me take control sometimes, you did once, but you stopped me saying you was gone come too quick, well damn, I should not be upset, this is some good pussy, and I understand you got to protect your feelings too, like you said, so I did not bring it up". He replies, "lmao, the sex was really good". She replies, "yea, it was good while it lasted, glad to make you laugh while I am expressing how I feel", threw up the deuces and hit send.

He replies, " it is not like that, I am laughing at the way you said baby... I like our friendship, and do not want to mess that up." She responds, "well, it is messed up, I no longer view you as just a friend, so, with that being said we should just part ways you know". "Do not treat me like that he replies, she did not respond, she had ended it. She wanted no more and had no more to say!

9/26/17

From this day forward, Kelli realized that she could not keep seeing him, no talking, or texting! It was over, a clear sign from God. "You get a thrill out of it, you are thinking all wrong! Do not go and do it again, or through it again. I am talking about heartache! Yes, I said it. It used to give me a thrill, I do not know why, but it was as if it was meant to be, a quick joyride, a game that only I knew about, I must stop, it is not who I am, nor who I want to be. "Tell me you hate me than", was one of my favorite lines in past relationships. You had to convince me that you did not love me! Sounds strange I know, I am making faces just writing it. But, seriously my mind was that fucked up when it came to love. I have felt love before, it was the best, but afterward, the worst hurt I have ever felt when my heart breaks. That shit hurt so bad, because after a while of pretending I started taking shit seriously, then would get mad, and have to cut him off. Is it normal to feel this way? My heart is so very deceiving!

I do not follow often what my mind says, it is a battle, one of many! "My hormones are fucking raging, I will not call you any more after this", Kelli started to text, but she deleted it before she pressed send. She studied his number really hard before she deleted it and the text thread, but she did not block him yet. Her pussy is still wet, but she does not want nothing from him, but some dick. She feels like these niggas now, like why you just cannot fuck without catching feelings, but she would back up too if a dude was treating her like a piece of ass. It tickles her, as she laughs and writes. Okay is he is blocked, unless he calls or texts right now. She will check her blocked messages two times before she went to bed. As she writes, she sees that it is not funny. "Bitch you need a dildo, or a man. You cannot keep playing games with people, it is not fair, you would not like it if it was the other way around. So, stop playing, he is not ready, and you are not either! "But we can grow together", is what she says, "but no one wants that though, I am crazy to think we can grow together. Why lead me on in conversation, oh wait, that is a whole different relationship", she is mad bad. She is at war with herself! How is this possible?

9/28/17

"I just want love. I want to love my man, and I want my man to love me just as much. I never really had that, a long, and strong relationship. I am tired of the games and the bullshit! It is time for a different prayer. I must change my ways and how I view love". 10/10/17

"Man, this dude must think I am a moron!" Kelli writes. See she was not even going to write about him anymore, because she no longer cares, and she had just ended this "fuck friendship" with Jason. "I wanted sex and that is what I got, but men talk about how females be in their feelings, this dude stays in his, more than I stay in mine. Or maybe, he is pretending, either way I am not fucking with him, he is doing too much, I am not with the lies and trying to run game, all that bullshit he be talking, I am not trying to hear it. We can talk about real life shit, goals, adventures, hobbies, music, politics, anything interesting. He trying to figure out since I have not contacted him, and the only time we communicate is when he contacts me. He wants to know if I am fucking with somebody else, he just did not want to ask me. But see I would prefer that he just asks me, but men and their pride. He did not want to seem jealous or anything, but he gone fuck around and get hurt, because I do not want him. He texted if I had some ice, I knew right then and there that this was his bullshit as reason to get into my house, but yes, I have some ice. He called when he was at the door he asked for a hug, okay you need a hug, let me get this ice out the freezer for you, but then he goes and sits on my couch, you see I made a choice at that moment like okay Kelli, do not flip out on this man, maybe he wants to talk about something, but he did not ask or anything, to come and sit on my couch, and I was in the middle of doing something, and he had to wait, he should have asked about coming over to chill, I would have told him that this is not the right time. "Just like you claim you been busy all day, so do I", I said, as I gets over to my couch after I finished up and gives him the ice tray since he has a cup. I go sit on the couch apart from him. He got a bottle of brown liquor and done pour him up a drink, I do not drink anymore. He is really acting, I just sat and watched like wow this fool done lost his mind, I am still fully dressed, changed out of my work uniform, after a nine- hour shift at the hospital, not to include the three hours travel there and back together, into my shorts and kept on the shirt I wore under my uniform, before he even got here. He trying to kiss on me, "eew, no! Sit over there, and I thought you was so busy working all day, Why do you have on clean socks, slippers, boxing shorts, and a Randstad t shirt, talking about you just got off and you tired, but still trying to fuck? Come on man even at Randstad you cannot wear that t-shirt, or those slippers" and he says he was helping someone move, "and if you are helping someone move all day, after work, you are doing it in slippers? And when you lifted your shirt I seen a lot of bumps on your stomach that was not there before", she says. "I am good on you, even after you get tested. I just got tested two months ago, even though I was not sexually active". Some diseases are dormant (sit inside you for years without you knowing). I will not risk it because condoms cannot protect you from everything, plus I had just got tested again that day.

Then you just told me you were messing with other women too, so "no, you cannot have any of my goodies". I started this and now I am ending it. I do not want you or any more of your sex! God sent you, he will send another, but that is not my focus right now, if I keep having sex with you it will cause me to feel something deeper eventually, as well as risking my health even though we never sexed without protection. I can tell that you are feeling some type of way, yea I remember feeling like that many times before, I pray that you get to where you want to be in life. We will see one another when we see one another" is what was said to him.

"I have been down this road before, I know a broke nigga when I see one. First of all Jason, I peeped game from the moment you opened your mouth. (Laughing Hella hard to myself). I texted him earlier and ask if I could get some weed when he got off work, that is how he ended up on my couch. He claims that he had been working all day but texting me all day today and yesterday as well, I guess after being apart he misses me, but fuck that, and fuck him! I told him that I did not want anything serious, and he says that he does not want anything serious either, so we both were cool with what we had going on. My thing is the type of friend he wants me to be, I am not that person anymore. I will tell you the truth and most likely than none, the truth will hurt, I hate telling myself the truth sometimes, but it feels better than walking around telling myself lies. Being honest with myself brings me joy, because there is no other me. I am honored to be me. My faith in God has carried me a long way, it is my turn to step up!

and do my part. There is no waiver, I have no other choice. I must love me, even if no one else ever does (I am truly loved) I must believe in me and have faith in myself that I can achieve all that God has directed me to do. I will not give up, I will not continue to give in. I will push forward. I am at the highest in life I have ever been, when it comes to making money, but I handle my finances so poorly, my credit score is getting better thanks to this helpful law firm. But Jason is trying to change my focus, not gonna happen. Leave me alone, I don't want it. Maybe this is karma".

10/20/17

"This war I keep fighting in my head is hard, no wonder God said to give it to him, because me alone trying to fight it, I often get defeated. I am now at peace with my mind. I act on what I need to and allow God to come and do the rest just as I should. I am forever grateful".

11/12/17

"Guide me, oh dear Lord, I do not know what you want me to do. I do not know what you want from me. I know that it is not this what I am doing daily now. Kelli continues, "I am lost, and I have been for awhile now. I need you help. I am trying to stay strong for my children, but I am getter weaker and weaker. I need your strength to show up Lord. Right now! The things that I am not doing for myself! The things I am doing for me, are not for my benefit, neither is it healthy for my mental, my physical, my emotions, or my feelings. Now that I mention it, it may very well be my feelings, I feel bad and sorry for me, pity for what has happened to me. I must get through this pity, despite what is going on, and regardless of how I feel. I must change the way I feel about me. Well, how do I do that? I have no energy. I am happy and sad at the same time, I never thought this could be, but I may have very well predicted this lost and confused state. I cannot see ahead past this, and that is what I need help on. I want to cry out to you, but I do not want my children around when I do it, but they are always around. Even if I allow them to go outside, I am afraid that they would walk back in too soon, and one did, the day before yesterday. She caught me on the floor crying out to you, so when I heard her coming, I asked her about her doll. This was not a coincidence that the cleaning crew had just picked it up for trash, so I went to get it from them. Wow, what made me ask about that doll? I do not know, but I wish it would come back and have me ask a few questions to myself or give me some answers to the questions I do have. What am I supposed to be doing with my life? I am satisfied with nothing and that should not be. I want somethings, but these things I want are not quite clear, well some are, but the steps to get there, starting over from the bottom, again is not what I wanted, but I remember speaking this into existence, I should not have done that. From now on, I will not speak horrible things into my life. This is my world, I will put in only good, so that only good may return to me. I cannot be perfect, God has made that clear, but when I do what is right, He will come near. A new routine must take place, so I can snap out of my old ways, and see new days. Because even as the days go by, there is no change in me, the same things I feel bad about doing, I continue to do them. This must stop! I need help Lord, this is my cry.

Admitting the truth is bad, it brings me down. How further down can I get? I am afraid to find out, yet I do nothing to try and stop it. It has taken over me, this cloud of confusion, having mixed feelings about every single thing in my life. My mind is rambling while at a standstill. Fear has overcome me, and it is here to cause damage, self-destruction, and mindless behaviors. It gives me reasons as to why I should continue to feel guilty and down. I do not want this anymore. I am trying to get rid of it, but how? Self-talk out loud is not my best friend is not my best friend, more like, "oh I heard of it, tried it a few times", but it makes me feel crazy. Maybe it is what I am saying, I need to talk to me, and lift me up, but I cannot do it alone, I need you Lord. Guide me back to you. Tell me and help me to know what my true underlining is. How to do what it is that you want me to do? What do you want me to do? I am sorry that I smoke, and drink coffee, and alcohol, and not enough water. I am sorry that I give in to these horrible things so easily. I feel bad that I should know better, well I do know better, but where is it? How do I get to better? I know it is somewhere. I want it. Why must I constantly struggle to find it? Why must I help to bring me down, do I not have enough enemies? I am most own worst, and that part of me, I want dead. How do I kill it? It is so loud, I want it to be quiet, but my methods are not working. I am saved because I believe Jesus died for me. This war between his race is killing me, but why should I let it get to me. I know he is not that white man society is portraying him to be. I am of his image, does that mean he looks like me. He is in me, just as I am in him, why must his voice be quieter than them. I wasted all my money on everything that is not good for me and my children. It kills me inside to know that what I did with my money was not right, yet I did it again today. And I tell myself every day, that today will be my last, but when the morning comes, it is the same thing, a year had gone by now, and I still smoke. This is harder than before. When I tell myself that it is going to get better, I turn right back around to show me that it will not. But I believe that it will, that is why I am calling out. I am sick of me! This is not me, but it is. I am bound with flesh, with this carnal nature that I do not want, simply because it is much harder to re-gain control, now that I have lost it. I need you to help me convince me to do better. I want peace in my mind again. I want to feel joy once more. It is coming soon, do not take too long. I do not want to self-destruct. Come save me now oh dear Lord. Now is the time! Why must I continue to wait? I am not even sure what it is I am waiting for anymore. I want to live now! I am tired of waiting, but, if I must wait, help me to enjoy it, and live through it, I need to get through it, your way. My ways are not better, nor will they ever be. I want to see and get to this better side of me. I turned around because I needed to bring you with me Lord. This path is too hard. I thought that I needed to bring me down, to find you, but you were up, so I had to turn back around, and bring me up, but it was not until I got down there, that I realized how much I needed you. I feel foolish because I ran away when it got hard, so now that you are back, I need you to strengthen me, and come with me so that I may return and face my fears, this time pushing through them. No more focusing on how, but more focused on you, because your ways are mysterious, and unexplained, but they work for the good, and that is what I want. So, if I just do my part, for instance, I want a healthier body with a nicer shape, I know that I must work out every day, and that laying and sitting all day will not get me there, but when I work out, I get tired so fast, then comes the excuses, no more excusing myself. I know that it will not happen overnight. I must find strength in you, and the energy to get it done, even if it is 30 minutes a day. I must commit, and that is doing my part. I believe that you will show mw results once I put the work in, and this is with everything in my life. I must work for it. Help me to get over that fear of doing my part. Why am I afraid? And just because I am afraid, does not mean I should let it stop me. How do I not fear? I need balance Lord. I need you in every area, in every day of my life. Do I stay here, or move back home? I hear me saying go where ever you want to go. But where do I belong? I want you to tell me, or is this you? My heart says home, but my heart is so deceiving, I do not want to listen to it. It has mis-lead me so many times before, so until I get my mind right, I am stuck. Come unstick me, so that I may be free. I know you can do this, help me to do this, show me where to go, what I should know, and what to do once I get there. Train my mind, set it, help me to keep it set, and not wander away into the dark".

11/14/17

"Every morning for the past three or four days I have been waking up with songs in my head. This morning it was Usher, "There goes my baby". Is this sign? If, so what does it mean? I am looking for me, but I cannot decipher the truth behind it all. I say I am going to change and some days I succeed, but everyday I still have my coffee and black and mild in the morning. This is the one routine that I want to change the most, but the more I try, the harder it gets. Why when I say that this is my last, I start new every morning, with the same routine? Well not every morning, the other day, I did follow my new routine, hot lemon water at night, but that was the only night. Why can I not get right? Must I train my body to follow my mind? I speak these new things out loud, but not as often as I should. I say them mainly in my head or write them. It is time I preach to myself, maybe that will help. Get down and dirty with the truth out loud every day, that should create change. I need to let go, maybe I miss it, or maybe I will just get over it. Lord help me!"

How bad do I really want to quit?

12/20/17

Kelli needs to allow people to help her. When she first moved to away, she lived in a hotel for three weeks, a shelter for three days then moved into her apartment, all on her own. She is happy to be free. This time she got it right, all that planning helped, "there is no more me stopping me", she declares. She even went to church two weeks in a row and although nothing has changed, and she does not like church, she knows, feels and can see that change coming, and soon too, so she must prepare herself to be able to accept it. "To prepare, I must be happy with me, I am for the most part, especially since I have been working hard with working out, and eating better, I have not eaten any meat since October, and no pork in seven years. I am happy, that I am being a great mom, learning, and doing things that I enjoy, although there are a few things that I still enjoy doing, like having wine and smoking, but now I do not do them as often. I have changed my focus to things that will help me, rather than break me, this new feeling that I am feeling is good, no more small dreams, they are much bigger now, I accept them, and focus on them. I know I can do it and although I feel afraid at times I am still going to constantly work towards my goals, taking the necessary steps to achieve them. The number one thing is prayer and faith, then comes the action. While doing it at first was difficult, not to mention the lack of motivation I desired from certain people, I have found a way to motivate and push myself. Now that I am doing that, I know that I am not alone. I heard a voice sounding just like me telling me to move on and keep going and that is exactly what I am doing. It is a great feeling to finally see me, the me I had been ducking and dodging for so long, is finally coming out and I love it. I am empowered, and it feels great to empower others it started with my siblings and friends, then my children, once I became a mother, people I hardly knew were even feeling me, and now it is my turn. I love me, I love how I have grown mentally over this year and now it is time to continue in action and reach even bigger goals. I am excited to start this new journey in my life, I know that it requires a whole new level of me and I am arriving, I am almost there, just a few more steps. I got to keep going it is coming, push, do not quit, keep it up, you got this! Get it Queen! What they say "slay baby slay" yes, babygirl, there you are! Wow, look at you! Doing the things you planned to do, working and accomplishing goals, seeing your dreams come true. "Who would have known that it was all just in my mind, the mind that I had control over all this time, and that all I had to do was change my focus, and instead of putting so much energy into thinking about what I did not want, I put that energy into what I did want, and it is happening, better than I imagined. I changed my focus, and it changed my life".

12/28/17

Even though I am in the same place physically, my mind has grown. I feel better! My mind is taking me to great places, and my body follows. This world I live in is free for me to cast down awesome visions and act on them. Creativity is endless, just because something does not exist, does not mean it cannot be created into existence. My mind does wonderful things for me. It helps me to see clearer each day, to focus on what I want, and what I want tends to focus back on me. It is a wonderful feeling, very much so that I admire it, and myself.

12/30/17

Take a walk on the bright side, and stay there for a while, try to make it last forever!

www.ingramcontent.com/pod-product-compliance
Lightning Source LLC
Chambersburg PA
CBHW052112070526
44584CB00017B/2454